Claudia Schiffer

Memories

This book is dedicated to those I love . . .

To my father and my mother who gave me the gift of life and who have guided my steps.

To my sister and my brothers who make me laugh and keep my feet on the ground.

To the photographers and the fashion designers who gave me the chance to share their dreams.

To my friends and my fans who have unfailingly been there, supporting me.

CLD

Mandarin Hardback

Claudia

Ellen von Unwerth

Schiffer

1975

The pupils of a nursery school in Rheinberg, a small German town near Dusseldorf.

4

But where is Claudia hiding?

Everything began

On the 25th of August the first-born baby of Gudrun and Heinz Schiffer took her first breath in Rheinberg, Germany, a small town near Dusseldorf. Later, the Schiffers would give their daughter Claudia the company of a sister, Ann-Carolin and two brothers, Stefan and Andreas, making a balance of two boys and two girls within the Schiffer brood.

With four mischievous, spirited children, discipline was a necessity in the Schiffer home. Claudia remembers the skill her parents brought to the task of setting limits, instilling values and laying down the rules in an atmosphere of affection and encouragement. Among the values Gudrun and Heinz taught was the priority of family: family came first. No matter how busy Dr Heinz Schiffer was with his work as a lawyer, time was always set aside for the children. And while Heinz worked during the day, Gudrun was home to manage the household and act as the children's confidante and, on occasion, to referee spats. Even today, when Claudia needs to discuss something or just wants to talk, regardless of the topic, she turns to her mother. Indeed, Claudia has placed the overseeing of her business affairs in the hands of Gudrun, her most trusted advisor, preferring – in Schiffer tradition – to keep the important matters squarely within the family domain.

One day this little blonde girl will grow up to be great.

Rheinberg is never far from her thoughts. Her birthplace is her home and haven. No matter where she is, whenever she can, she'll get on a plane and return to her home, her old bedroom, the pleasures of family and childhood friends. At home in Rheinberg her life resumes the comforting pattern of her past. There, the simplicity of life reigns and the pressures of celebrity are forgotten. Rheinberg's citizens have never changed their earnest ways, and when Claudia the Supermodel returns, they treat her with the gentle warmth they show everyone, regardless of their status in the world. Here, Claudia can walk down the street like everyone else. It's good to be home!

'**X**' *marks the spot* . . . **Stefan, one of Claudia's brothers.**

The little heart-throb: **Claudia remembers this little boy . . . They were always in the same class at primary school. She tells us, with amusement: 'I loved Bernd for years . . . but even back then I was taller than he was!'**

From chrysalis to butterfly. . .

"I desperately wanted to be shorter when I was a teenager and less of a beanpole. Everything I wanted to change about myself is exactly what others liked about me later."

C laudia Schiffer a supermodel? No one ever imagined it – least of all Claudia! During her early years as a teenager all that mattered to her was family, friends and schoolwork. Although she

was certainly lovely, Claudia was known as much for her mischievous sense of humour as for her looks. Fortunately she has retained both, since in her profession, as she'd be the first to admit, a sense of humour is indispensable.

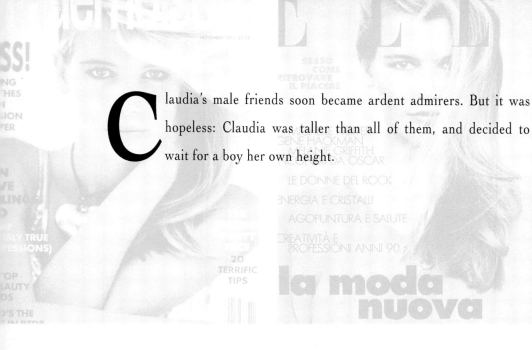

Claudia's male friends soon became ardent admirers. But it was hopeless: Claudia was taller than all of them, and decided to wait for a boy her own height.

Here, Claudia is on vacation in Majorca with Uta, her best friend. The pair of fourteen-year-olds announced that they were actually seventeen-year-old fashion models, to anyone who would listen. The boys were taken in (or pretended to be), and this fib would become a reality for Claudia within three years.

"When I was little, I hated having my photo taken.
If I was asked to smile on demand,
I just wanted to
disappear . . ."

O n her first composite, as it is known in the trade, her height was only 5'10". The girl from Rheinberg still had growing pains.

First photo

Marie-Françoise Prybys

sessions

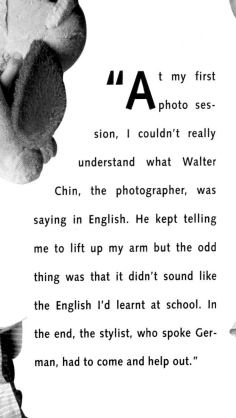

Marie-Françoise Prybys took Claudia's first test shots. The superb results were enough to win over Odile Sarron, *Elle*'s casting director.

"At my first photo session, I couldn't really understand what Walter Chin, the photographer, was saying in English. He kept telling me to lift up my arm but the odd thing was that it didn't sound like the English I'd learnt at school. In the end, the stylist, who spoke German, had to come and help out."

Walter Chin

First photo sessions

Claudia at seventeen: the age when one dreams of the future. A career as a model did not figure in her dreams, however. She was barely interested in fashion and didn't even know the name of any of the photographers.

"This is my very first cover. I wore barely any make-up. Gilles Bensimon, the photographer, was doing a series of photos in Mexico of young, up-and-coming models, and it was a chance for me to go on a trip. To be photographed in a country far from my home and have the picture appear on the cover of *Elle* – that I was really becoming a model began to sink in. When the magazine came out I only bought two copies, one for me and one for my mother."

One night at a club in Dusseldorf with friends, a tall, dark-haired man approached her. He said he was the director of a modelling agency. Would she come to Paris?

Claudia was amused by the whole thing and was sure it was a joke. The man gave her his card and explained that he was quite serious, he was not a flirt or a prankster, and asked if he could telephone her at her parents' to discuss things further.

Gilles Bensimon

Her first interview in *Elle*.

14

done. When they returned to Rheinberg they agreed that Claudia could go for a day – but just a day – to do the necessary test. If she liked it and the test results showed promise, she would be permitted to return.

An appointment was made with a young photographer named Marie-Françoise Prybys, who had a studio in Paris. Fate again intervened. The test photographs were superb. The day of the test was also the day Claudia met Aline Souliers, the woman who was to become her agent and life-long friend.

Within weeks *Elle* magazine called Claudia to Paris for a shoot. It was to be the first of many, and soon she was increasingly in demand.

The next day, the man telephoned to invite Claudia and her parents to lunch to discuss a possible career for their daughter.

They had a lot to talk about. Was it a good idea for Claudia to become a model at seventeen, when she was doing so well with her studies? Would such a career disrupt her life, taking her from family and friends?

The director reassured the Schiffers. He explained the route taken by a beginner, the test shoot, the first sessions, the discipline involved, the uncertainty of succeeding. They discussed it with Claudia, who expressed an interest in trying it out. Her mother and father were protective but cautious about not stifling their children's ambitions; they went to Paris without Claudia to see exactly how things were

By choice Claudia continued to live at home in Rheinberg, working only at weekends, determined to complete her schooling with good grades.

Upon finishing school, she travelled to Paris to learn French and to work in the city of fashion. She came to love Paris and her career, which flourished with astonishing speed. But success did not go to her head. She knew her profession was fickle and subject to the vagaries of whim and luck. She knew that her rise might halt at any moment. Claudia decided that if it did, she would go home, go to law school, and become a lawyer like her father. Meanwhile she spent each weekend in Rheinberg, where her parents were encouraging but concerned.

"**F**or the first time in my career I posed for some provocative pictures. Antoine Verglas put me at ease and I knew with him behind the camera there was nothing to worry about: the photos would not be exploitative or cheap. They came out on the cover of *Photo* magazine, and the reaction was very enthusiastic."

Antoine Verglas

Claudia reassured her parents that the work was enjoyable. She was able to travel and see parts of the world she might not otherwise have visited.

Certainly she had a knack for the work: even though her career was just beginning, two women were certain she would have a brilliant future – her agent, Aline Souliers, and *Elle's* casting director, Odile Sarron, who confided that from the moment she first saw Claudia, she knew she was looking at someone destined to become a star.

Time has ratified their faith. Claudia Schiffer is one of the most famous models ever. But success has not poisoned her with conceit. She retains the discipline, intelligence and humour she showed as a child, doing her best without regard for fame or success, concentrating on progressing a step at a time.

When, for example, she began posing regularly for French *Vogue*, she dreamed of appearing on the cover. When that happened, she dreamed of posing for the American *Vogue*, which also happened: "My dreams got bigger like that, little by little."

"These photos were taken in Morocco on one of my very first shoots. I was visiting new countries all the time."

Today, the girl who just a few years ago went to Paris to learn French and take a photo test is fluent in three languages. Her agent gets over twenty offers a day and must, in consultation with Claudia, choose among them, organizing a life that travels from one end of the world to the other.

This is the first photograph of Claudia taken by Ellen von Unwerth. Ellen's talents were destined to play a role in the meteoric success Claudia would inevitably obtain.

The ad campaign for Guess Jeans turned Claudia into a star in the States, completing her rise to the top of her field as one of the most recognizable and sought-after women in the world.

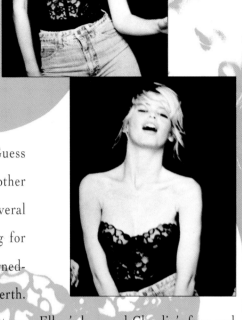

Being chosen for the Guess campaign was another stroke of fate. For several months Claudia had been posing for *Elle*, where she met model-turned-photographer Ellen von Unwerth. There was a perfect chemistry between Ellen's lens and Claudia's face and form. Understandably proud of their collaborations, Ellen showed some of the photos to Guess president Paul Marciano, who frequently hired Ellen for Guess shoots. Marciano immediately saw in the photos the blend of innocence, insouciance and insinuated fire that would be perfect for the Guess campaign. Claudia was chosen. Ellen oversaw her transformation from a girl with a fresh, unstudied look to a vamp with heavily kohled eyes and drop-dead cleavage.

"I could hardly recognize myself when I saw the photos," Claudia explained. "I was startled and amazed at first, but I loved them!"

From the outset of the campaign people wanted to know more about the blonde on the posters. The Press began to print articles about Guess girl Claudia Schiffer, and Marciano decided to make her the face for Guess perfume. A tour of the States was organized with Claudia as the spokesperson. Despite the media attention, Claudia was surprised to find people staring at her on the streets of New York. The normally unflappable New Yorkers could not stop looking at the woman from the Guess ads. The campaign was a turning point in her career.

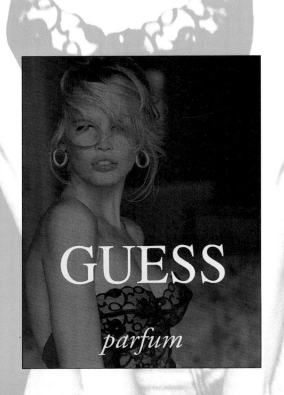

GUESS
parfum

Ellen von Unwerth

Star

And Karl Lagerfeld makes her his muse. . .

Claudia, photographed by Karl Lagerfeld in Berlin: the powerful impact of an extraordinary team.

Karl Lagerfeld

The Meeting

Herb Ritts's now famous photographs of Claudia struck Karl Lagerfeld with the force of a revelation. The legendary designer felt compelled to find the tall girl who wore Chanel's clothes as if they had been designed for her. Lagerfeld knew he had to see her – whoever she was – model the Chanel designs for him in the fashion shows.

When Claudia heard of Lagerfeld's plans she was terrified. "I can't," she said. "I'm too shy to be in a fashion show. I don't even walk like a model, with that feline grace." Her excuses meant nothing to Karl Lagerfeld, who had the confidence in Claudia she herself would acquire only with time. It was the ineffable power and grace of her personality that fascinated him, and he decreed that the supreme honour of modelling the wedding dress would be hers.

VOGUE'S EYE VIEW

PARIS COUTURE

À la recherche du temps Bardot: a Parisian dream of a blonde, a boudoir, a boy on a motorcycle and a couture wardrobe fit for a star

Yves Saint Laurent little black dress

Herb Ritts

Lagerfeld's plans for Claudia were nearly stymied when she came down with the flu – three days before the all-important show was to occur. Still, when the day arrived Claudia managed to drag herself from bed and, despite fever and chills, she staggered into the elegant designs. Just before making her début, her first entrance ever, Claudia told herself, "Well, if this turns out to be a fiasco I'll go back to the camera where I belong."

She stepped on to the catwalk. That step was like a strange tonic that wedded her with fate and erased all the flu symptoms in an instant. The press and public gawked, stared in amazement and applauded. Never before had they seen a cooly smouldering, mischievous blonde in a Chanel show. Immediately afterwards people rushed backstage to find out who this girl was and where she had come from.

Chanel changed Claudia and Claudia changed Chanel: the sober suit became less staid, and the proper dress became short and sexy.

Karl Lagerfeld

29

The Muse and the Creator

Karl Lagerfeld was convinced that Claudia, like a great actress who can play any role, could transform herself into virtually any persona or look. Her face and body permitted her to convey the essence of Lagerfeld's most subdued or extravagant designs. Thus Lagerfeld launched Claudia and Claudia continued to provide his inspiration. Their collaboration became a close friendship as the two Germans (a rarity in the world of fashion) chatted in their mother tongue as they worked.

It was also the first time a blonde had been chosen for Chanel's designs. Traditionally, since the days of Coco Chanel herself, a typically Parisian type – dark-haired and highly refined – had been chosen. It was Lagerfeld who had the foresight to put aside tradition and choose the tall blonde who was unselfconsciously lusty and filled with cool heat.

On the occasion of her birthday, Karl Lagerfeld used his talent for drawing ('Dear Claudia, I wish you a wonderful new year of life. Your Karl'), a sign of the closeness which still exists between them.

In the Rue Cambon there was soon talk of "before Claudia" and "after Claudia". Her appearance in the designs was a watershed event. After Claudia, Chanel was no longer the sole province of society women. Even teenagers began to dream of wearing something from Chanel – with jeans! Like Claudia Schiffer. The elegant, sober label had been revitalized.

The First Steps in the Spotlight.

Claudia's first fashion show had been a success, but for her once was enough. She felt that the shows weren't right for her.

But those who were there for her début found her unforgettable. She quickly became known throughout the fashion world as "La Schiffer". The Press sought her out for interviews, asking what she did in her spare time, where she was from, what she ate, what she read. Her agent was surrounded by letters and faxes.

She and her agent sorted through the requests for her services, choosing the designers she most admired: Valentino, for his extraordinary elegance, Gianni Versace for his daring conceptions of an avant-garde fashion.

ALAÍA

VALENTINO

VALENTINO

CHANEL

CHANTAL THOMASS

Long live the catwalk!

VERSACE

35

Under a spell . . .

Gilles Bensimon

When she arrives for a photo shoot – always with punctuality – she is invariably without make-up. The hairdressers and make-up artists begin to work on her, teasing her hair, putting it up, or tying it back; underlining her eyes, outlining her lips, emphasizing her skin's natural colour. Bare-faced, she radiates her

Beppe Petrone

Walter Chin

Patrick Demarchelier

preternatural purity. It is a purity so true that even in the heaviest make-up she is sexy but never vulgar.

At home, she spends no time in front of the mirror: "In my profession we spend too much time looking at ourselves. So when I get home the only time I look in a mirror is when I'm brushing my teeth."

She didn't purchase a make-up kit until she was twenty. By then she had been a top model for nearly three years.

The key to Claudia's beauty is the blessing of nature, an unaffected disposition and a will that is unyielding. When she is not working, Claudia wears little, if any, make-up – a hint of eye-liner and mascara, and that's all. She does not crave coffee (even the smell of which she dislikes), cigarettes or alcohol. Her one vice is chocolate, which she indulges from time to time. But after the craving is sated she returns to light meals of fresh fruits and vegetables, and she never exceeds her ideal weight of 126 pounds.

Antoine Verglas

KARL LAGERFELD

From the start of her career, photographers have remarked about her professionalism. For her part, Claudia knows that the photographer is the model's ally and collaborator, and she has enormous respect for their craft.

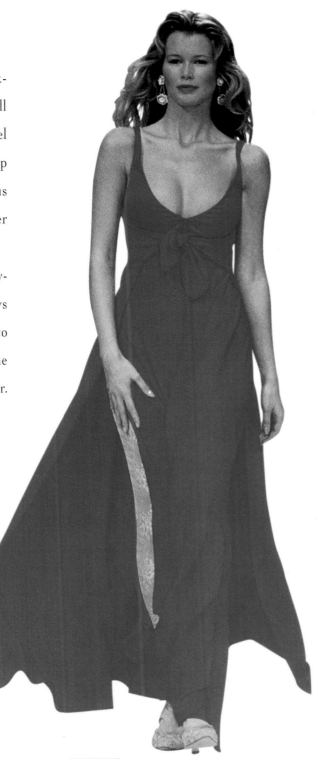

laudia has conquered the stage fright she once felt about walking on the catwalk. But the camera is the medium she still prefers. An extraordinary rapport develops between a model and photographer during the course of a shoot, not unlike the relationship between a skilled actor and the director. Words almost become superfluous as the collaborators understand intuitively what each needs from the other to make the shoot a success.

This rapport is one of the things that makes her profession so enjoyable, and when it's not there, the work can be gruelling. In the early days of her career, Claudia worked with a photographer who was barely civil to her. Claudia said she would never work with him again. Even though he was famous, she wasn't, and her refusal could have jeopardized her career. Claudia, however, has never sacrificed sincerity for fame.

VALENTINO

VALENTINO

From almost Chanel to pure Chanel

Claudia evinced a sense of style entirely her own even as a teen-ager, realizing that there was more to dressing than jeans and T-shirts. She had an intuitive way of putting together certain colours and even fabrics that people had not thought of as complementary, often wearing jeans and an elegant jacket, a look that is now standard for men and women alike but, just a short time ago, had not been seen.

She still chooses and assembles her wardrobe with intuitive ease and imagination, combining the creations of bold young designers with the classic clothes of the great couturiers. Wherever she goes, she effortlessly conveys her unerring sense of style, a sense she will not compromise.

Her now world-famous face and distinctive style get recognized wherever she goes, but she is still far too unaffected to slink around in dark glasses with a hat pulled low over her face, ostentatiously trying not to be noticed. Her watchwords are honesty, simplicity and ease.

At the age of one and a half, Miss Schiffer already had a certain Chanel look about her.

The idea for this unusual photo, which was part of the Chanel publicity campaign, came to Karl Lagerfeld when he was gazing at his own umbrella (opposite page).

Karl Lagerfeld

Nude fishing with her friends . . . nude posing on the beach for the photographer.

Pose nude? Yes, but there are limits! She implicitly trusts the great professionals. As the self-respecting German that she is, Claudia has never had a complex about nudity. On the beach, children walk around naked and women topless. Claudia grew up in that environment, with a liberated body and a mind totally at ease.

Now that she is famous she has had to learn to protect herself, to draw a veil in order to shut out prying eyes, and for the first time in her life she has taken to wearing a bikini top on the beach. All summer long, dozens of paparazzi photographers pace up and down over miles of sand in the hope of catching a glimpse of Claudia, preferably nude. Ruthlessly using powerful zoom lenses, they litter the gutter press with shoddy, stolen shots of her. Would they enjoy the same treatment?

So, a nude shot? Yes, but not just any nude shot! She dares to adopt the sexiest poses with the most seductive smiles . . . but she never gives anything away, she never actually uncovers anything. And she will only do this in front of a photographer of her choosing!

Claudia is the baby on the left, but at this point it's still possible to mistake her.

Patrick Demarchelier

Being a supermodel also means taking the unexpected in your stride.

Someone at Revlon decided to put Claudia on roller-blades, but she had never even ice-skated. On the day of the shoot she gamely strapped on the skates and forged ahead with courage but not much balance. Fearing that she might fall, the team stood ready to catch her if she wobbled. Fortunately, she did not need their much-appreciated assistance.

Karl Lagerfeld

The Monte Carlo sea is icy in November, and her outfit does not afford much protection from the cold! But all we see is the perfection created by the world's most gifted model in collaboration with her photographer, not the discomfort involved in producing the arresting shots.

The viewer is shown a stunning image, never the toil that went into its creation.

47

January 1992:

Claudia Schiffer signed the biggest modelling contract of the century when Revlon chose her to be its ambassador.

Bruce Weber

In the space of a few years, Claudia Schiffer had become the symbol of beauty and femininity. Already on the cover of fashion magazines, she could be seen from then on making the front page of newspapers. What more could a big cosmetics firm wish for, then, than to have an exclusive contract with "the most beautiful woman in the world"?

Claudia hadn't changed, but she had matured. She was surer of herself, more determined. She possessed all the qualities of a perfect ambassadress: a responsible outlook, charm, meticulousness and a great smile. Experience had taught Aline, her agent, that Claudia was ready to take on the adventure of that contract.

Securing a beauty contract is no easy matter. There are many candidates and few winners.

Revlon was interested in Claudia but they are a company with very exacting standards. The executive wanted to see the star, speak to her, see exactly how she behaved in front

of a television camera, see how she responded to journalists. The negotiations lasted almost a year. Claudia passed every exam with great success.

But this victory had its price, and that price was to forgo any involvement with other makes of perfume and make-up. She was wedding herself to Revlon for several years. But she was a happy bride and went wherever duty called her: to press conferences throughout the world, to photoshoots for campaigns, to promotional films, and various galas.

On the 10th January, 1992, when she signed the contract at 625 Madison Avenue, New York, her hand wasn't shaking but her heart was racing. She had just signed the contract of the century. For how much? Only five people in the world know, and they're not telling.

Claudia has a pet project: her calendar.
Once a year, it's her turn to create something!

Claudia's calendar is the one project over which she exerts complete control, from the make-up she will wear to the type-face used on the calendar. Always the perfectionist, Claudia then spends months studying the photographs, selecting and rejecting and re-selecting them. Her hard work seems to be paying off: when the first calendar came out in 1992, it was an instant success. Bookstores could not keep it in stock. The following year was even more successful, as the calendar was distributed world-wide.

1992, Antoine Verglas/Achard & Associates – 1993, Ken Nahoum – 1994/1995, Gilles Bensimon

The image of Claudia the water nymph is an irresistible reminder of the pin-up stars from the 1950s, but in a wilder and more irreverent version. As with everything she does, Claudia does not evoke a tradition, she reinvents it.

The integrity Claudia inherited from her parents and honed at home influences her professional decisions and her approach to the work. She prepares meticulously for press conferences and television commercials, regardless of their importance. When she was preparing to film a few seconds of a commercial for Revlon, Claudia asked for all the background information on the company's new products and its marketing strategies for them.

She has also refused to advertise any product she doesn't believe in, regardless of how much money she is offered. As she puts it, "If money or fame had been the only motivating forces behind my decisions, you would have seen me posing for anything and everything."

Despite her efforts, occasionally she will still read an interview with Claudia Schiffer that she never gave, or hear that she was seen in a place she has never been to with someone she has never met. Such little evils nettle, but only slightly, allowing her to retain her even temper. She understands that such falsehoods are an occupational hazard.

Gilles Bensimon

Gilles Bensimon

Gilles Bensimon

Antoine Verglas

Antoine Verglas

Ellen von Unwerth

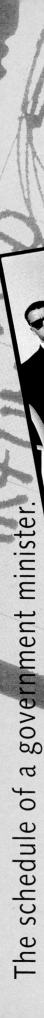

The schedule of a government minister.

Claudia's schedule is fixed a year in advance. It has to be to accommodate a life-style that is absolutely chaotic. It is not unusual for her to cross the equator three times in two days. Sometimes things get sacrificed along the way, like sleep. But Claudia willingly gives whatever her profession demands. Her long-time friend and agent Aline Souliers does what she can to make sure Claudia can rest as much as possible between jobs. This isn't always easy: one day's work requires several days of preparation. The camera captures the glamour but not the effort that goes into producing it.

Claudia accepts everything that her profession asks of her. Her agent does everything she can to ensure that Claudia's life is as little tiring as possible. In the evenings, they spend hours on the phone planning for the future.

56

TODAY

DATE
MAY 24, 1994

MON **TUE** WED THU FRI SAT SUN

SCHEDULE / NOTES

CHANEL UHREN

7:00 Aline anrufen (Vogue us in Rom oder in Paris?)

8:30

18:00

WICHTIG: Karl Lagerfeld Mittwoch morgen anrufen !!! (PHOTOSHOOT IN MONTE-CARLO FÜR "Marie-Claire")

GYM
19:00 TRAINER Kathy! Broadway dance center Studio 3

20:30 DINNER mit Stephen Poe (CBS/FOX)

NOTIZEN: →
1. soll Videos schicken!
2. wer ist der Produzent?

CALL D.C. IN L.A. ♥

COMMENTS ① Geburtstagsgeschenk für Stefan kaufen! ② Landmark Kathy Scott / Promotion!

CLAUDIA SCHIFFER 1994

Ellen von Unwerth

57

The many faces of Claudia.

She is not one of those disingenuous stars who crave recognition but garishly strive to go unnoticed in attention-getting disguises. Claudia knows that hundreds of fans wait for her wherever she is due to appear. When asked for an autograph Claudia is always gracious and indeed grateful for such a show of interest.

To the girl from Rheinberg, it is still amazing that so many of her admirers know the details of her life and career. Meeting her fans is one of her great pleasures, and she makes sure she remains accessible to the public. "No matter how famous you are," she notes, philosophically, "there are always people who don't know who you are or that you even exist."

Hideaways

Hans Feurer

Claudia missed her first communion because of the flu. No one made a fuss. This official photo was postponed for two weeks, and a fully recuperated Schiffer was introduced to one of the most meaningful rituals of her faith.

Now that she is an adult, life is less easily rescheduled. People have definite expectations of her. Even if she is running a temperature of 104°, a photo shoot cannot be postponed. She has done a fashion show with a broken toe, photo shoots with fevers, colds and even food poisoning. In her profession, if you call in sick, no one believes you.

She has been blessed with an extraordinary beauty. As one admirer remarked, "Claudia Schiffer is one of life's joys." But Claudia owes her success to more than the happenstance of good looks. It is her attitude toward life that separates her from thousands of other beautiful women in the world. Claudia has not permitted success to swell her ego or cause conceit. In a profession dedicated to the flesh and the physical, Claudia's upbringing has helped her to hold on to values that never age or fade: don't deceive yourself or others; respect everyone; lead a happy, contented life.

Ellen von Unwerth

She has always paid as much attention to preserving her inner convictions as she has to maintaining her looks. Her life is a reflection of the inner integrity that flows from her wholeness, harmony and radiance.

With the family.

When Claudia's parents saw her first magazine covers they were surprised and proud but they had no idea what the future held. They never tried to persuade or discourage her ambitions, choosing instead to encourage Claudia to follow her instincts and heart in finding her path. Since her meteoric rise, Claudia's parents have discovered a world that had been alien to them. To help their daughter keep track of a busy life, her mother maintains a meticulous record of everything Claudia has done and looks after her business affairs. Whenever she gets time to go home, Claudia and her brothers and sisters pick up where they left off, as if she had never been away at all. It's important to her to see her family as often as she can. Her little brother Andreas, who was only five when she left for Paris, tells her how his classmates pester him for her autograph. The precocious young man has announced plans to start charging for his famous sister's signature. So far, however, the pint-sized entrepreneur has not put the plan into effect.

EASTER '81
in Rheinberg

CHRISTMAS '92
with my dad

CHRISTMAS '79

CHRISTMAS '90
with my mom

CHRISTMAS '91

my ♡-sister Ann-Carolin

my mother Gudrun

my brother Stefan

CHRISTMAS '87
with my brother Stefan

my father Heinz

that's me!

my "little" brother Andreas

Claudia is devoted to Majorca, where the Schiffers have a vacation home for the summer. Her childhood memories of laughing giddily, of learning to dive, of romping with her brothers and sisters, are revived each time she goes back.

Her passions are reading, sports and friends.

A selection of literature . . . She has her favourite authors whose books she reads over and over again.

During a brief stopover there's time for a quick reunion with Uta, her childhood friend. Claudia loves travelling to cities where old friends live and catching up on things over long, leisurely dinners. She also loves hearing their messages on her answering machine: "Claudia, we know you're terribly busy and we're thinking of you all the time."

Claudia enjoys sports for the sheer pleasure of doing them as much as for the exercise. Unfortunately, she rarely has time to ski or ride.

Another favourite city is Monaco, where Claudia keeps a *pied-à-terre* she escapes to when she gets a respite from the routine of life in airplanes and hotels. There, in her sun-filled apartment, Claudia can find peace and solitude. She occupies these moments of privacy with sleep – an activity often in short supply – with painting, with reading her favourite authors (Balzac, John Irving, Max Frisch), and with exercise, of course.

Home at last she can forget, at least for a while, cameras and catwalks.

Kako Topura is one of Claudia's favourite artists. Topura's paintings of mischievous cats adorn the walls of her apartment.

At Claudia's, there is a story behind every single object.

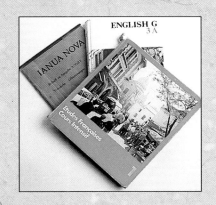

He apartment is cosy and full of her singular charm. When it comes to decorating, Claudia is guided entirely by caprice and instinct, and all the objects – some worn but cuddly teddy bears, a starfish, a few butterflies – have a history only Claudia knows.

R elaxing in Monaco, Claudia clowns with the photographer.

Metamorphoses

How is it that she is able to embody 90s woman in all her various forms?

Unexpected
covers

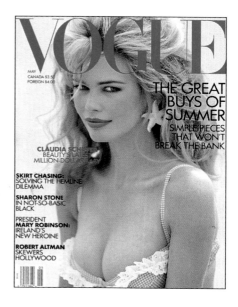

She flew from New York to Miami Beach just for the afternoon to get a cover shot. The shoot, with Patrick Demarchelier, went pretty much according to plan, but the people at *Vogue* liked the photos so much that, to her surprise, they used them for two consecutive covers.

Every week a new image of Claudia appears on a magazine cover in the United States and Europe. To paraphrase the old saying, "Behind every picture there is a story . . ."

"This is one of my first, and favourite, covers. It was shot in the Seychelles by Hans Feurer. He took a series of photos of me wearing a highly elaborate hairstyle that took hours to create. After the shoot Hans was packing up his equipment, and I took down my hair. Hans suddenly unpacked all his gear and took another shot. That last photo is the one they used for the cover!"

Feline Serendipity (above, left): "This little cat wandered into the studio during the shoot for *Glamour*. It wasn't supposed to be in the photos but as soon as I picked it up Santé d'Orazio shot a whole series of pictures of the two of us. In the end, the cat made the cover."

Above, right: "I love the irony of being so heavily made-up to achieve 'the natural look!'"

Right: "This photo was shot by Gilles Bensimon for my 1994 calendar. It's a case of the photographer displaying a hidden talent as a designer. Originally the swimsuit was quite conservative, without that high leg cut and plunging neckline. Gilles thought it wasn't sexy enough, and he came over with his assistant's scissors and made a few impromptu cuts. As a first attempt at clothing design I think it's a stroke of genius!"

"When I arrived at his studio in New York, Steven Meisel – who loves to bring spontaneity to his shoots – said, 'Hey, let's try something different.' He rooted around and chose a dark wig. I put it on as a goof, just for fun. Neither one of us thought this photo would become a cover."

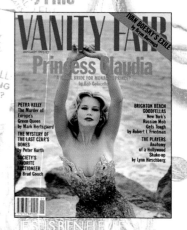

Fragile or elegant, a *femme fatale* or a dangerous

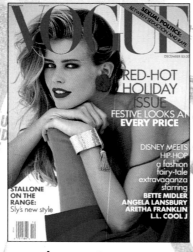

Lolita, a provocative adventuress or

an insolent dandy, Claudia embodies the hidden

sides that are in all of us.

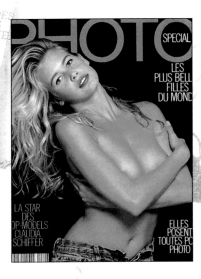

A Venus for the 90s.

Her mere
image sparks
extraordinary
rumours and
dreams.

Torrid by day . . .

Ellen von Unwerth

For American *Vogue,* **photographer and long-time friend Ellen von Unwerth photographed the supermodel on the back of a vintage car in a frilly bikini, transforming Claudia into a 1950s pin-up.**

and cool by night.

Karl Lagerfeld

Karl Lagerfeld wanted to see if he could transform the spontaneous and open girl into Claudia the Ice Queen. With her hair pulled into a tight bun and her shoulders bare, she was able to create the illusion he sought. But this was one persona that did not come naturally, a fact of which she was suitably proud!

At home in any decade

A harsh urban setting for a Chanel ad. Claudia assumes an impassive pose, parodying a 1960s London hippie.

... and in the country.

In the country, for Chanel, Claudia looks entirely innocent. Note Karl Lagerfeld's mischievous touch: the underwear drying on the clothes line.

Wild . . .

Really wild in the Bahamas in front of Antoine Verglas's camera. This page from the 1992 calendar sent millions dreaming. The muse of the great fashion houses can also be sensual.

Antoine Verglas

. . . and mischievous.

Margaretha Olschewski

This is from her first job, in Thailand. Despite her inexperience, Claudia remained relaxed in front of the camera.

Margaretha Olschewski captured this puckish smile on film.

Impish adolescent . . . and elegant lady.

Ellen von Unwerth captured a rare moment: Claudia collapsing on the sofa, having just danced until she was breathless.

Right: the spirited young girl can also play the refined lady. This photo was taken on her first meeting with Karl Lagerfeld, who put her in his show and helped launch a career.

A star from the 1920s . . .

CHANEL HAUTE COUTURE

. . . a young bride for the 1990s.

Hair today . . . wild, soft and flowing, plaited, or Hollywood glamour.

Captured by the same photographer,

this is no act: absolute seduction?

There is no artifice: pure beauty?

Francesco Scavullo

Editorial Director: Agnès TOURAINE

Art Editor: François HUERTAS

Editor: Jean-François LACAN

Text adviser: Marceline SOULIERS-LERALE

Interviews by Catherine SIGURET

English editorial consultant: Ted BLUMBERG

My warmest thanks to the photographers whose work is reproduced here, taken especially for this book or for advertisements: (*in alphabetical order*):

Tito BARBIERIS, Gilles BENSIMON, Walter CHIN (Scop *Elle*), Patrick DEMARCHELIER, Hans FEURER, Marc HISPARD, Karl LAGERFELD, Ken NAHOUM, Margaretha OLSCHEWSKI, Beppe PETRONE, Marie-Françoise PRYBYS, Herb RITTS, Francesco SCAVULLO, Ellen von UNWERTH, Antoine VERGLAS, Bruce WEBER.

My warmest thanks to the following reportage photographers: (*in alphabetical order*):

Steve ALLEN (Gamma Liaison), Philippe Georges ANDRE, Alain BENAINOUS (Gamma Liaison), Eric BOUVET (GLMR), Sandra FOURQUI et Alexandra ACCART, Luc NOVOVITCH (Gamma Liaison), Nicolas SEGALEN, Daniel SIMON (Gamma), William STEVENS (Gamma).

Aline! Thank you for having faith in me, for your talent and for your friendship. Love, Claudia.

Thank you to Jacques LEHN, for having made it possible for me to do this book.

First published in Great Britain 1995 by Mandarin Hardbacks, an imprint of Reed Books Ltd
Michelin House, 81 Fulham Road, London SW3 6RB and Auckland, Melbourne, Singapore and Toronto.

This edition published 1995 by Mandarin Hardbacks, an imprint of Reed International Books Ltd, Michelin House, 81 Fulham Road, London SW3 6RB

© Text Claudia Schiffer 1995

© Editions No 1, Hachette Group Livre, Paris 1995

ISBN 0 7493 2262 4